compiled by
Dorothy Baldock

SALMON

Index

Bacon and Beans   23
Bacon Fraise   32
Celery Soup   41
Cheese Tartlets   17
Chicken Galantine   37
Devizes Pie   44
Dower House Fruit Chutney   38
Druids Cake   19
Ham Mousse   11
Malmesbury Pudding   5
Marlborough Cake   26
Matrimony Cake   14
Onion and Apple Pie   31
Onion Broth   10
Pickled Green Cabbage   40
Potted Chicken and Ham   22
Rhubarb and Mixed Peel Jam   16
Roast Saddle of Lamb and Plum Sauce   7
Seed Cake   47
Stilton Soup   34
Stir-in Pudding   20
White Cake   35
Wiltshire Buttermilk Cake   43
Wiltshire Lardy Cake   28
Wiltshire Market Day Dinner   13
Wiltshire Porkies   4
Wiltshire Pork Pie   25
Wiltshire Sausages   8
Wiltshire Tatties   46

Cover pictures *front:* Salisbury Cathedral from the meadows
back: Poultry Cross, Salisbury
Title page: The Market Cross, Malmesbury

Printed and Published by Dorrigo, Manchester, England. © Copyright.
All rights reserved. No part of this publication may be reproduced, stored in a retrieval system or transmitted, in any form or by means, electronic, mechanical, photocopying or otherwise. Images/Recipes J Salmon Ltd

Wiltshire Porkies

A popular farmhouse supper dish.

4 oz. flour	1 lb. pork sausagemeat
Salt	4 apples, peeled, cored and cut into rings
1 egg, separated	Parsley sprigs

Mix the flour and salt together in a bowl, then add the egg yolk with sufficient cold water to make a thick, smooth batter. Set aside. Form the sausagemeat into about 12 balls and dust very lightly with a little seasoned flour. Whisk the egg white until it stands up in peaks and fold into the batter. Dip the sausagemeat balls into the batter and deep fry in hot oil until golden brown. Remove from the oil, drain well on a piece of kitchen paper and keep hot. Dip the apple rings into the remaining batter and fry for a few minutes. Drain well on a piece of kitchen paper and keep hot. Reserving a few sprigs for garnish, dip the remaining parsley into the batter and fry for a minute. Drain well on a piece of kitchen paper. Serve the 'porkies' on a hot dish, surrounded by the apple rings and fried parsley and garnished with the reserved parsley sprigs. Serves 4.

Malmesbury Pudding

*If preferred this pudding can be served the
old-fashioned way, straight from the basin.*

6 oz. self-raising flour	Cold water
Pinch of salt	4 oz. butter
3 oz. shredded suet	8 oz. soft brown sugar or
3 oz. sultanas or raisins	demerara sugar
Grated rind of a lemon	1 dessertspoon lemon juice

Sift the flour and salt together in a bowl, then add the suet, fruit and lemon rind and mix to a stiff dough with cold water. Roll out on a lightly floured surface and use two-thirds to line a well buttered 1½ pint pudding basin. Cut the butter into cubes and place in the basin, then spoon over the sugar and sprinkle on the lemon juice. Cover with the remaining pastry and seal the edges very well. Cover with buttered greaseproof paper and kitchen foil and tie down. Place in a steamer over a saucepan of boiling water and cook for 2 to 2½ hours, topping up the water as necessary. To serve, turn out the pudding on to a warm, deep serving dish and cut into slices, spooning over the syrupy sugar, butter and lemon pond. Serve with whipped cream. Serves 4 to 6.

Roast Saddle of Lamb with plum sauce

A Wiltshire festive dish which is ideal for a dinner party

**A saddle of lamb, wiped   Oil or dripping   Black pepper
2 sprigs of rosemary   ¾ pint lamb stock
Salt and black pepper   8 tablespoons port**

PLUM SAUCE
**1 lb. plums, stoned and chopped   4 oz. sugar
½ pint white wine vinegar   1 tablespoon fresh mint, finely chopped**

Set oven to 350°F or Mark 4. Place the saddle in a roasting tin and brush with oil or dripping. Dust with black pepper and place the rosemary sprigs on the joint. Roast, allowing 20 minutes cooking time for every lb. in weight, and baste from time to time. When cooked, place the joint on a serving dish and keep hot. Drain off the excess fat from the roasting tin, then add the stock. Bring to the boil, stirring to take in the tin juices, then season, stir in the port and heat through. Pour into a gravy boat and serve with roast potatoes and vegetables as preferred. *Sauce:* Place the plums in a saucepan with the sugar and vinegar and bring to the boil. Simmer until the plums are soft, then mash with a fork to produce a rough purée. Stir in the mint, spoon into a sauce boat and serve hot with the Saddle of Lamb.

The Tithe Barn, Bradford-on-Avon

Wiltshire Sausages

An excellent easy meal which if preferred can be grilled rather than fried.

1½ lb. lean, boneless pork	Scant ¼ teaspoon ground cloves
½ lb. shredded suet	¼ to ½ teaspoon chopped fresh sage
½ lb. fresh breadcrumbs	(if desired)
Salt and white pepper	1 egg, beaten
Scant ¼ teaspoon ground ginger	Flour
Scant ¼ teaspoon mace	Fat for frying

Mince the pork, then stir in the suet, breadcrumbs, seasoning and sage (if desired). Combine very well and add sufficient beaten egg to bind the mixture. *Note:* the beaten egg is used to hold the sausage mixture together, as it is not being placed in skins or casings. Form into sausage shapes and coat with a little flour. Heat the fat and fry the sausages until brown. Serve with vegetables. Makes about 10 to 15 sausages.

Onion Broth

A nourishing and tasty Wiltshire broth.

1 oz. butter   4 large onions, peeled and chopped
1 stick celery, wiped, trimmed and chopped
1 carrot, peeled and chopped
1 or 2 rashers streaky bacon, rind removed and diced
1½ to 2 pints chicken stock   1 oz. oatmeal (if desired)
Salt and black pepper   Pinch of grated nutmeg
Pinch of dry mustard powder
4 sprigs parsley, 1 sprig thyme and a small bayleaf, tied together
1 medium potato, peeled and diced   3 to 4 oz. Cheddar cheese, grated
Fresh chopped parsley for garnish

Melt the butter in a saucepan and fry the onions, celery, carrot and bacon until softened but not browned. Stir in the stock, the oatmeal (if desired) and the seasoning and herbs. Bring to the boil and simmer, covered, for 15 minutes. Add the potato and simmer for a further 15 to 20 minutes. Remove the herbs, pour the broth into warmed bowls and top with the grated cheese. Garnish with chopped parsley and serve with chunks of crusty bread. Serves 4.

Ham Mousse

Wiltshire is very well known for its hams and the finest is the Bradenham with its distinctive black rind.

2 eggs, separated   ½ pint prepared white sauce, cooled
Salt and black pepper   ½ teaspoon ground nutmeg
3 tablespoons dry sherry   1 oz. gelatine
1 tablespoon hot water   ¾-1 lb. ham, finely minced
1 hard boiled egg, sliced
and
watercress or parsley sprigs for garnish

Blend the egg yolks with the white sauce, then reheat, very gently, stirring all the time. Do not allow the sauce to boil or it will curdle. Add the seasoning, nutmeg and sherry and combine well. Dissolve the gelatine in the hot water and stir into the sauce, then add the ham. Remove from the heat and stir well. Cover the surface with a butter paper, to prevent a skin forming and leave to cool. Whisk the egg whites until they stand up in peaks and fold into the mixture. Well rinse a 2-2½ pint mould in cold water, turn the mixture into it and place in the refrigerator for 2 hours or until set. Turn out and garnish with slices of hard boiled egg and sprigs of watercress and parsley. Serve with tomatoes and green salad or with buttered, boiled potatoes and green peas. Serves 4 to 6.

Wiltshire Market Day Dinner

4 pork chops, trimmed and cut in half if very large
2 pig's kidneys, skinned, cored and sliced   2 large onions, peeled and sliced
1 large apple, peeled, cored and sliced   1 teaspoon fresh, chopped sage
Salt and black pepper   1 lb. potatoes, peeled and sliced
½ pint pork stock   ¼ pint dry cider (optional)
A walnut of butter   Chopped fresh parsley for garnish

Set oven to 325°F or Mark 3. Place the chops in a deep casserole and top with layers of sliced kidney, onion and apple. Sprinkle over the chopped sage and season well. Cover with an overlapping layer of potatoes, then pour in the stock and the cider, if desired. Cover and cook for 2 hours. Remove the lid, dot the potatoes with butter, return to the oven and allow to brown slightly for a further 20-30 minutes. Serve garnished with parsley. Serves 4.

The Town Hall, Wootton Bassett

Matrimony Cake

If preferred, the honey can be replaced by golden syrup

**8 oz. prepared shortcrust pastry   4 apples, peeled, cored and sliced into rings
4 tablespoons lightly crisped breadcrumbs
3 tablespoons sultanas   1 tablespoon chopped peel
½ teaspoon ground nutmeg and ginger, mixed together
The juice of 1 lemon, rind of half a lemon and 1 slice of lemon
2 tablespoons clear honey   A little milk for glazing
A little sugar for sprinkling**

Set oven to 400°F or Mark 6. Roll out the pastry on a lightly floured surface, divide in half and use half to line a lightly greased and floured 8 inch flan tin. Cover the base with overlapping apple rings, then mix together the breadcrumbs, fruit, peel, spices and lemon juice and rind and sprinkle evenly over the apple rings. Place the slice of lemon in the centre, then drizzle over the honey. Dampen the edges of the pastry then place the remaining half of the pastry over, trimming the edges neatly and sealing well. Brush with a little milk to glaze and prick lightly with a fork. Bake for 15 minutes, then reduce the heat to 350°F or Mark 4 and bake for a further 15 to 20 minutes, until the pastry is golden. Sprinkle with a little sugar and serve hot with whipped cream. Serves 4 to 6.

Rhubarb and Mixed Peel Jam

Spiked with a little ginger, this is a traditional Wiltshire jam.

3 lb. rhubarb, trimmed, wiped and chopped
3 lb. preserving sugar
1 small to medium piece root ginger
3 oz. chopped mixed peel

Place the rhubarb in a bowl and sprinkle over the sugar. Cover and leave in a cool place for 24 hours. Then strain off the liquid that has accumulated, pour into a saucepan, bring to the boil and boil for 10 minutes. Bruise the ginger and add to the rhubarb in the bowl, then sprinkle over the mixed peel. Pour the liquid over the rhubarb, leave to cool, then cover and allow to stand for a further 24 hours. Transfer the mixture into a very lightly buttered preserving pan. Bring to the boil, then boil rapidly, stirring frequently, until setting point is reached, skimming as necessary. Allow to cool a little, remove the piece of ginger and pour into clean, warm jars. Cover and label. Makes 3 to 4 lbs.

Cheese Tartlets

Up until the beginning of the First World War, Wiltshire produced its own notable cheese which was similar to Gloucester.

10-12 oz. prepared puff pastry	½ pint milk
2 eggs	Pinch of salt
1 oz. butter	Pinch of English mustard powder
1 oz. flour	Pinch of cayenne pepper

4 oz. mature Cheddar cheese, grated

Roll out the pastry thinly on a lightly floured surface and cut into 3-3½ inch rounds. Use to line 18-24 greased and floured tartlet tins, trimming the edges neatly. Separate the eggs. Melt the butter in a saucepan, stir in the flour, then add the milk a little at a time, stirring to produce a smooth sauce. Bring to the boil, stirring, and boil for 2 minutes. Allow the sauce to cool slightly. Set oven to 425°F or Mark 7. Beat the egg yolks into the sauce and reheat, but do not allow to boil or the sauce will curdle. Add the seasoning and stir in the grated cheese. Whisk the egg whites until they stand up in peaks and fold into the mixture. Divide evenly between the tartlet tins and bake for 10-15 minutes until golden and puffy. Serve hot.

Druids Cake

Stonehenge on Salisbury Plain has long been associated with the Druids. The monument is, however, centuries older than the Druids and this cake centuries younger!

6 oz. butter   6 oz. caster sugar   3 eggs, beaten
A few drops of vanilla essence (if desired)
½ lb. flour   2 teaspoons baking powder
Prepared white glacé icing, flavoured with vanilla (if desired)
Halved glacé cherries, angelica diamonds and hazelnuts for decoration

Set oven to 350°F or Mark 4. Grease and line an 8 inch square cake tin. Cream the butter and sugar together in a bowl until light and fluffy. Add the beaten eggs and vanilla essence (if desired) and whisk until well combined. Sift together the flour and baking powder and fold into the mixture to form a soft, dropping consistency. Spoon into the cake tin and smooth over the top. Bake for 30 to 40 minutes until lightly golden and springy to the touch. Cool in the tin for 5 minutes, then turn out on to a wire rack. When completely cold cover the top with glacé icing and decorate with glacé cherries, angelica and hazelnuts.

'Stir-in' Pudding

Any fruit can be used for this pudding, but rhubard or gooseberries are the most traditional

12 oz. self-raising flour   Pinch of salt
6 oz. butter
½ lb. prepared fruit – gooseberries, topped and tailed, or rhubarb, trimmed and chopped
4 oz. sugar   1 small egg, beaten   A little milk

Sift the flour and salt together in a bowl, then rub in the butter. Stir in the prepared fruit and the sugar. Then stir in the beaten egg and sufficient milk to form a fairly thick mixture. Spoon into a well buttered 2 pint pudding basin and smooth over. Cover with buttered greaseproof paper and kitchen foil and tie down. Place in a steamer over a saucepan of boiling water and cook for 2½ to 3 hours, topping up the water as necessary. Turn out on to a warm serving dish and serve accompanied by hot gooseberry or rhubarb sauce or custard or cream. Serves 4 to 6.

An old corner, Lacock

Potted Chicken and Ham

1½ oz. butter
1 small onion, peeled and finely chopped
¼ lb. chicken livers
½ lb. cooked ham
½ lb. cooked chicken
2 tablespoons fresh chopped parsley

Salt and black pepper
Pinch of nutmeg
Pinch of mace
2 tablespoons brandy or chicken stock
Melted butter
Parsley sprigs for garnish

Melt the butter in a frying pan and lightly fry the onion until soft, but not browned. Add the chicken livers and fry until cooked. Drain off any excess fat and allow to cool a little, then mash the onion and liver well together. Mince the ham and the chicken separately and stir 1 tablespoon of chopped parsley into each, then season and add the spices. Lightly butter a potting dish or 4 to 5 individual ramekins and add layers of the liver, ham and chicken. Smooth over the top layer and sprinkle over the brandy or stock, then pour over the melted butter to seal. Place in the refrigerator until the butter is set. Serve, garnished with parsley and accompanied by fingers of toast. Eat within two to three days.

Bacon and Beans

This is a centuries old cottager's dish which made a little go a long way.

2 to 2½ lb. forehock of bacon, diced **Black pepper**
3 to 4 onions, peeled and chopped **Pinch of dry mustard powder**
½ lb. haricot beans **A bayleaf**
Water or stock

Place the haricot beans in a bowl of cold water and leave to soak overnight. Next day boil in fresh water in a saucepan for 10 minutes and drain well. Layer the bacon, onions and beans in a saucepan, add seasoning and the bayleaf then pour over sufficient water or stock to cover. Cover the saucepan, bring to the boil, then simmer gently for 1½ to 2 hours or until the bacon and beans are tender. Remove the bayleaf and serve with boiled potatoes and cabbage or carrots. Serves 4 to 6.

Wiltshire Pork Pie

**12 oz. prepared shortcrust pastry   ½ oz. butter   1 onion, peeled and chopped
2 rashers streaky bacon, rind removed and chopped
1 lb. belly of pork, chopped   1 small cooking apple, peeled and chopped
2 to 3 oz. Cheddar cheese, diced   2 tablespoons chopped fresh parsley
1 teaspoon chopped fresh sage   Salt and black pepper
Pinch of dry mustard powder   1 egg, beaten
A small sprig of sage for garnish**

Roll out the pastry on a lightly floured surface. Divide in half and use half to line a lightly greased 9 inch pie plate. Melt the butter in a frying pan and lightly fry the onion and bacon. Add the belly of pork and cook for 15 to 20 minutes, stirring frequently. Allow to get cold, then stir in the apple, cheese, herbs and seasoning, adding sufficient beaten egg to bind the mixture. Set oven to 425°F or Mark 7. Fill the pie plate with the pork mixture and top with the remaining pastry, sealing the edges well and trimming neatly. Make a steam hole and decorate with pastry leaves. Brush with the remaining beaten egg to glaze. Bake for 15 minutes, then reduce the temperature to 350°F or Mark 4 and bake for a further 25 to 30 minutes, until the pie is golden brown. Serve hot or cold, garnished with sage. Serves 4 to 6.

Marlborough Cake

4 eggs **6 oz. flour**
½ lb. caster sugar **1 oz. caraway seeds**
A little sifted icing sugar

Set oven to 425°F or Mark 7. Place the eggs and sugar in a warm bowl set over a saucepan of hot water and whisk until the mixture is creamy and thick enough for the whisk to leave a trail when drawn across the surface. Remove the bowl from the heat. Sift the flour and fold half into the mixture, together with half the caraway seeds, using a metal spoon and combining well. Fold in the remainder of the flour and caraway seeds and spoon the mixture into a greased and floured 8–9 inch round cake tin. Bake for 10 minutes, or until the mixture is well risen and springy to the touch. Cool in the tin for 5 minutes, then turn out on to a wire rack. When cold, dredge the top with sifted icing cake.

Wiltshire Lardy Cake

Originally this delicious yeast cake would have been made with dough left over from a bread-making session.

½ teaspoon sugar	4 oz. lard
3 fl. oz. warm milk	4 oz. granulated sugar
1 teaspoon dried yeast	4 oz. sultanas and currants, mixed
¾ lb. strong white flour	½ teaspoon mixed spice
¼ oz. salt	1 oz. granulated sugar
¼ oz. lard or margarine	2 tablespoons milk

Dissolve the sugar in the milk, then sprinkle on the yeast and leave in a warm place until dissolved and frothy – about 10 minutes. Mix the flour and salt together in a bowl and rub in the ¼ oz. lard or margarine. Make a well in the centre and stir in the yeast mixture to form a firm, but not too sticky, dough. Turn out on to a lightly floured surface and knead until the dough is smooth – about 10 minutes. Form into a ball, place in a clean bowl and, covering with a clean teacloth, leave to rise in a warm place until it has doubled in bulk. Then knock back and knead on a lightly floured surface until the dough is firm – about 2 minutes. Then roll into a rectangle, about 10 inches by 6 inches. Cut the 4 oz. lard into flakes and spread one third of the lard on to two thirds of the dough. Then sprinkle over one third of the sugar. Fold up the uncovered third of the dough and the top third down to form a 'parcel', sealing the ends with a rolling pin. Give a half turn to the dough and roll out as before, adding the lard and sugar and half the fruit and spice before folding up again. Repeat this process once more, then roll out the dough for a fourth time, fold without any additions and roll out to fit a 7-inch square cake tin, well greased with lard. Cover with a clean teacloth and leave to prove in a warm place for 30 minutes. Set oven to 450° or Mark 8. Score the top of the lardy cake in a diamond pattern and bake for 25-30 minutes. Dissolve the sugar in the milk and boil until syrupy to form a glaze. Brush the glaze over the hot lardy cake and leave for 2 minutes, then remove from the tin and turn upside down on a wire rack over a plate to cool, spooning any lard or syrup left in the tin over the base of the cake. Serve upside down, cut into slices, either plain or spread with butter.

Onion and Apple Pie

If the pie is to be served cold, 2 to 3 oz. of grated or diced Cheddar cheese can be added with the onion.

**8 oz. prepared shortcrust pastry   2 onions, peeled and sliced
A little oil or butter   1 lb. cooking apples, peeled, cored and sliced
Salt and black pepper   ½ teaspoon chopped fresh sage
2 teaspoons chopped fresh parsley   1 to 2 tablespoons thick double cream
A little beaten egg to glaze**

Set oven to 400°F or Mark 6. Roll out the pastry on a lightly floured surface. Divide in half and use half to line a lightly greased flan tin. Sauté the onions in the oil or butter until soft, but still transparent, then drain well. Place half the apple slices on the pastry, and top with the onion. Season well then sprinkle over the herbs. Add the remaining apple slices, then drizzle over the cream. Top with the remaining pastry, sealing the edges well and trimming neatly. Make a steam hole in the centre of the pie and decorate with leaves cut from any pastry trimmings. Brush with beaten egg to glaze and bake for 30 to 40 minutes until the apples are cooked and the pastry golden brown. Serves 4 to 6.

The Parish Church, Mere

Bacon Fraise

*This popular breakfast dish uses a method of cooking
which dates back to the 15th century.*

**8 oz. streaky bacon, rinds removed
and cut into strips or pieces
½ pint prepared batter mixture, (the mixture may contain a little cream if desired)**

Set oven to 450°F or Mark 8. Fry the bacon lightly in a lightly greased frying pan. Transfer to a heated, well greased oven proof dish and pour over the batter. Bake for 20 to 30 minutes or until the batter is well risen and golden brown and crisp. Serve in wedges, very hot, with mustard and accompanied by grilled or fried tomatoes, if desired. Serves 4 to 6.

Stilton Soup

2 oz. butter   1 large onion, peeled and finely chopped
2 sticks celery, wiped, trimmed and finely chopped
1 carrot, peeled and chopped (if desired)
1 clove of garlic, peeled and crushed with a little salt
1 oz. flour   2 tablespoons white wine   1 to 1½ pints chicken stock
¼ pint milk   4 to 5 oz. Stilton cheese, rind removed and crumbled
Salt and black pepper   Pinch of grated nutmeg
5 tablespoons single cream   2 tablespoons fresh, chopped chives or parsley

Melt the butter in a saucepan and lightly fry the onions, celery and carrot (if desired) until softened but not browned. Add the garlic, then stir in the flour and cook, stirring, for 1 minute. Stir in the wine and the stock, bring to the boil and simmer for 30 minutes. Add the milk, Stilton cheese and seasoning and heat through, stirring, for 1 minute. Liquidise in a blender and pour into a clean saucepan. Stir in the cream and 1½ tablespoons of the herbs. Heat through, but do not allow to boil. Serve garnished with the remaining herbs. Serves 4 to 6.

White Cake

This pale sponge is sandwiched with rum-flavoured whipped cream.

**4 oz. butter   8 oz. caster sugar   1 lb. self-raising flour
Pinch of salt   A scant ½ pint milk   3 egg whites
½ teaspoon vanilla essence or the finely grated rind of a lemon
Double cream   A few drops of rum
A little sifted icing sugar**

Set oven to 350°F or Mark 4. Cream the butter and sugar together in a bowl. Sift the flour and salt together and add gradually, stirring between additions. Gently stir in the milk, then add the vanilla essence or lemon rind. Whisk the egg whites until they stand up in peaks and fold into the mixture. Divide the mixture between two lightly greased sandwich tins and bake for 20 to 30 minutes until springy to the touch. Turn out on to a wire rack and cool. Whip the cream until it holds its shape, then stir in the rum. Sandwich the cakes together with the rum-flavoured cream and dust the top lightly with sifted icing sugar.

Chicken Galantine

Galantine is a dish that is said to date back to Romano – British days. This modern galantine comes from Marlborough. If preferred, it can be served hot with vegetables.

**1 lb. prepared chicken breasts   1 lb. cooked ham
4 oz. breadcrumbs   2 tablespoons chopped fresh parsley
2 eggs   ¼ pint double cream   Salt and black pepper
¼ teaspoon nutmeg
8 rashers streaky bacon, rinds removed, and lightly stretched
Parsley sprigs for garnish**

Set oven to 375°F or Mark 5. Mince together the chicken and ham, then stir in the breadcrumbs and parsley. Beat the eggs together with the cream, add seasoning and nutmeg and stir into the chicken/ham mixture until well combined. Line a lightly buttered and base lined 2 lb. loaf tin with the bacon rashers, overlapping them slightly. Then spoon in the chicken/ham mixture, press down lightly and smooth over the top. Wrap over any protruding bacon rasher ends. Cover with buttered greaseproof paper and kitchen foil and tie down. Stand in a 'bain marie' and cook for 1 to 1¼ hours, removing the foil and greaseproof paper for the final 15 minutes. Cool slightly in the tin, then turn out and cool completely. Serve garnished with parsley, with salad and boiled potatoes. Serves 4 to 6.

The Garden Front, Wilton House

Dower House Fruit Chutney

½ lb. brown or preserving sugar
1 pint malt vinegar
½ lb. apples, peeled, cored and chopped
1½ lb. plums, stoned and sliced
¼ lb. raisins
½ lb. onions, peeled and chopped
¼ lb. carrots, peeled and chopped

1 teaspoon ground cloves
1 teaspoon ground cinnamon
1 teaspoon ground nutmeg
1 teaspoon ground allspice
½ teaspoon dry mustard powder
1 to 2 teaspoons salt
4 to 6 peppercorns, tied in a piece of muslim

3 tablespoons malt vinegar

The fruit and the vegetables should be weighed after preparation.

Place the sugar and the pint of vinegar in a preserving pan and bring slowly to the boil, then add the fruit and vegetables. Blend the spices and seasoning with the 3 tablespoons of vinegar and add to the mixture with the bag of peppercorns. Bring to the boil, stirring, then simmer, stirring regularly for about 1 to 1½ hours or until the chutney has thickened. Cool slightly, remove the bag of peppercorns and then pot into clean, warm jars. Cover when cold with non-metallic lids and label. Makes about 3 lbs.

Pickled Green Cabbage

This accompaniment to cold bacon and ham is less well known than Pickled Red Cabbage, but it is equally tasty.

**1 lb. firm green cabbage, trimmed and sliced
(the cabbage should be weighed after preparation)
1 medium onion, peeled and sliced   1 to 1½ tablespoons salt
1 pint malt vinegar   1 oz. pickling spice**

Dry brine the cabbage and onion as follows: Mix the cabbage and onion together and layer with the salt in a bowl. Cover and leave in a cool place overnight. Prepare the spiced vinegar as follows: Boil the vinegar and pickling spice together for 1 minute, then allow to cool. Cover and stand for 2 hours – longer if a stronger spiced vinegar is required – then strain. Rinse the cabbage and onion and drain very well. Pack into clean jars, pour over the spiced vinegar, cover with non-metallic lids and label. Store in a cool place and use after 2 to 3 weeks. Drain very well before serving with cold bacon or ham.

Celery Soup

**1½ oz. butter   1 head celery, wiped, trimmed and finely chopped
1 onion, peeled and finely chopped
1 rasher streaky bacon, rind removed and finely chopped
1 oz. flour   1 pint chicken stock   ½ pint milk
Pinch of caster sugar   Salt and black pepper
Pinch of grated nutmeg   5 tablespoons single cream
A little grated cheese –preferably red such as Leicester – for garnish**

Melt the butter in a saucepan and lightly fry the celery, onion and bacon until softened but not browned. Stir in the flour and cook, stirring, for 1 minute. Stir in the stock, bring to the boil and simmer for 15 minutes. Add the milk, sugar and seasoning and simmer for a further 15 minutes. Liquidise in a blender and pour into a clean saucepan. Heat through and stir in 4 tablespoons of cream. Heat through, but do not allow to boil. Serve with the remaining cream swirled lightly into each bowl and garnish with grated cheese. Serves 4.

Wiltshire Buttermilk Cake

This farmhouse fruit cake appears in various forms all over the country.
The Wiltshire version is richly spiced.

1 lb. flour	**4 oz. brown sugar**
1 teaspoon bicarbonate of soda	**4 oz. raisins**
½ teaspoon mixed spice	**4 oz. sultanas**
½ teaspoon ground ginger	**4 oz. currants**
¼ teaspoon ground cinnamon	**Grated rind of half a lemon**
6 oz. butter	**¼ pint buttermilk**

Set oven to 325°F or Mark 3. Grease and base line an 8 inch cake tin. Sift together in a bowl the flour, bicarbonate of soda and spices, then rub in the butter until the mixture resembles fine breadcrumbs. Stir in the sugar and fruit and lemon rind. Warm the buttermilk slightly, then stir into the mixture to form a soft dough, adding a little extra buttermilk if it is too stiff. Spoon into the tin and smooth over the top. Bake for 1 hour, then reduce the heat to 300°F. or Mark 2 and bake for a further 40 to 45 minutes, covering the top with a piece of kitchen foil if it appears to be browning too quickly. Cool in the tin for 5 to 10 minutes, then turn out on to a wire rack.

The Market Cross, Castle Combe

Devizes Pie

**1 lb. lean stewing lamb, in one piece   8 oz. English lean pie veal, in one piece
1 onion, peeled and quartered   1 carrot peeled and cut into chunks
1 small turnip, peeled and cut into chunks   1 stick celery, trimmed and cut into chunks
A sprig of thyme and a bay leaf   1 dessertspoon white wine vinegar
Lamb stock   2 oz. sliced tongue   2 oz. sliced ham   ½ oz. gelatine
2 rashers streaky bacon, lightly fried and cut into quarters
2 hard boiled eggs, sliced   4 tablespoons chopped fresh parsley
Cayenne pepper   Allspice   Salt and black pepper (if desired)
8 oz. prepared shortcrust pastry   Beaten egg, mixed with a little salt to glaze**

Place meat, vegetables, herbs and vinegar in a pan, then pour over stock. Cover, bring to boil and simmer for 20 minutes. Cool, lift out the meat and cut into slices. Strain stock and reserve. In a deep 1½ to 2 pint pie dish, arrange layers of meat, tongue, ham, bacon and eggs, seasoning each layer with a little cayenne pepper, allspice and parsley. Salt and black pepper can be added. Pour in sufficient stock to moisten well. Set oven to 350°F or Mark 4. Roll out pastry and line rim of dish. Dampen and cover with remaining pastry. Make steam hole and decorate. Glaze with beaten egg. Bake for 20 minutes, reduce heat to 325°F or Mark 3 and bake for further hour, covering if browning too quickly. Allow to cool a little. Heat remaining stock, sprinkle over gelatine and stir until dissolved. Pour into pie through steam hole and leave until cold. Serves 4 to 6.

Forty Four — Potterne near Devizes

Wiltshire Tatties

An old way of cooking large potatoes as a supper dish.

**4 large potatoes   4 level tablespoons brown breadcrumbs
4 oz. ham or cold cooked chicken, finely chopped
3 oz. butter, softened   2 teaspoons finely grated lemon rind
1 tablespoon fresh, chopped parsley   ½ teaspoon ground nutmeg
Salt and black pepper   Parsley sprigs for garnish**

Set oven to 350°F or Mark 4. Scrub the potato skins, dry with a piece of kitchen paper, then prick lightly with a fork. Dust lightly with a little salt and bake in their skins for about 1 to 1½ hours or until they are soft. Allow to cool, then cut a piece off one end of each potato. Taking care not to break the skins, scoop out all the potato flesh. Place in a bowl, then add all the remaining ingredients, mixing them together until well combined. Divide the mixture equally between the potato skins, then flatten the bases a little so that they will stand up. Place in a lightly greased baking tin and return them to the oven, increased to 400°F or Mark 6, for 15-20 minutes. Serve garnished with parsley sprigs. Serves 4.

Seed Cake

Seed or 'seedy' cakes were very popular in the Victorian era, being considered light, digestible (especially for children) and economical to make.

8 oz. flour
½ teaspoon baking powder
6 oz. butter or margarine
6 oz. sugar
3 eggs, beaten
2 to 3 teaspoons caraway seeds
3 to 4 tablespoons milk

Set oven to 350°F or Mark 4. Grease and base line a 1½ lb. loaf tin. Sift together into a bowl the flour and baking powder. Cream the butter and sugar together until light and fluffy, then add the flour and the eggs alternately, combining the mixture well. Stir in the caraway seeds and the milk and turn into the tin. Smooth over the top and bake for 1¼ to 1½ hours, covering the top with a piece of kitchen foil if it appears to be browning too quickly. Cool in the tin for 5 minutes, then turn out on to a wire rack. Slice and serve plain or toast and serve spread with butter.

METRIC CONVERSIONS

The weights, measures and oven temperatures used in the preceding recipes can be easily converted to their metric equivalents. The conversions listed below are only approximate, having been rounded up or down as may be appropriate.

Weights

Avoirdupois	Metric
1 oz.	just under 30 grams
4 oz. (¼ lb.)	app. 115 grams
8 oz. (½ lb.)	app. 230 grams
1 lb.	454 grams

Liquid Measures

Imperial	Metric
1 tablespoon (liquid only)	20 millilitres
1 fl. oz.	app. 30 millilitres
1 gill (¼ pt.)	app. 145 millilitres
½ pt.	app. 285 millilitres
1 pt.	app. 570 millilitres
1 qt.	app. 1.140 litres

Oven Temperatures

	°Fahrenheit	Gas Mark	°Celsius
Slow	300	2	150
	325	3	170
Moderate	350	4	180
	375	5	190
	400	6	200
Hot	425	7	220
	450	8	230
	475	9	240

Flour as specified in these recipes refers to plain flour unless otherwise described.